The Shoestring Business Manual

Copyright © 2013 by Michael F. Castleberry

All rights reserved. No part of this book, except for use in any limited review, but including the reproduction or utilization of this work in whole or in part may be reproduced, scanned or distributed in any printed or electronic form, including, but not limited to, photocopying and recording or in any information storage or retrieval system, currently known or of future development without written permission of the author.

"Eating the Elephant"

This manual is based upon the premise that anyone wanting to start a business is not only ready to devote the time and energies necessary to make it a reality, but also a success. For that reason, the author highly recommends that you not get in a hurry; there is always plenty of time to do it right. In fact, one of the major reasons for failure is the attempt to grow too big too fast. There's an old adage: How do you eat an elephant? The answer is: a bite at a time. So, if you want to grow big, do it in small, manageable steps.

You already have a business in mind or you wouldn't be reading this manual. Further exploration of that idea will lead you to the *right* choices.

The very first step is to decide just how likely you are to be considering a business that is really viable and, just as important, can you actually perform the tasks necessary to make it happen? Follow all the steps in this manual, page after page, and you'll answer that question along with determining just exactly how to make your dream business a reality.

Is your business choice based on what you really can do or is it just an idea? This is the most important determination you are going to make; like building a house, the foundation must be solid before you start putting up walls. The next section is guiding you to decide what business you should choose.

Step 1:

Collecting Potential Business Choices

Print the next page and keep it with you at all times until it is complete. Take your time, even several days or weeks, to write down your ideas for a business-you think you could operate. This means you know something about the actual performance of providing a particular product or service to a client. Don't worry about record keeping and taxes and such; we'll cover that and more later. All you're concerned about right now is if you can actually fill a client's need. It isn't necessary to place them in any particular order.

Look around as you drive and notice those businesses that can be performed by a single person and consider each of them against your skills. Pay special attention to larger, more complex businesses that you feel fall within your general skill set. Observe them until you can identify the separate parts and then pick one of those parts that you think you could do.

  For instance, a large lawn care company might till, plant, mow, trim, weed, spray, mulch, and irrigate a given property. You note that the landscape installation and plant care is more than you can do, but the irrigation is something you could maintain. On the list you are carrying with you, write "irrigation maintenance and repair."

Possible Businesses

1. _____
2. _____
3. _____
4. _____
5. _____
6. _____
7. _____
8. _____
9. _____
10. _____

Step 2:

Organizing Your Choices

When you have about ten businesses on your list, begin to imagine yourself actually performing the business transaction. Picture yourself meeting with the client for the first time, performing the service and collecting your money. Think about this carefully.

After you have thoroughly thought through all the ten businesses on your list, write down the business you feel the most confident about next to the number "1" on the following list. Write the business you feel the least confident about next to the number "10." This establishes the most likely choice and the least likely choice. Now, write the business you feel you could do, but aren't totally sure of next to the number "5." Using these three choices as guidelines, fill in the remainder of the original ten in their order of confidence in your ability to fulfill the actual job for a client, whether it is providing a product or a service.

1. _____

2. _____

3. _____

4. _____

5. _____

6. _____

7. _____

8. _____

9. _____

10._____

Look this list over carefully and set it aside for several days, then look at it again. Make any position changes you feel are appropriate. Remember: this is a long race, not a sprint.

Remember:

***Doing it right is far better than doing it fast.**

Step 3:

Making the Final Choice

Once you have the final list in the order you think is the best, purchase three steno type notebooks. Number them as shown below. On the front cover of one, print in large letters the first business on your list. On another of the notebooks, print the name of the second business on your list. The third business should be printed on the cover of the last notebook.

Put your list of ten potential businesses aside; do not destroy it. You put a lot of time and thought into those choices and each is on that list for a reason. They may become viable choices at some time in the future.

While the foregoing steps may seem so simple as to insult an average adult's intelligence, remember that most businesses fail due to not thinking through the business choice and the ability of the entrepreneur to provide a competent level of service to a client. The second reason, which we will come to later, is letting overhead grow too high so that it consumes too much of the business income.

You now have three empty notebooks numbered one, two, and three. Take any one of the three and open it to the first page. Now, using only your own thoughts about how you would actually service a client, begin to write the steps you would take. Don't be concerned about putting them in order. That comes later. For right now, just write down as many of the details as come to mind.

As an example, imagine your business is to perform plumbing repair. Your list might initially look something like this:

1. Ask what the problem is that they need corrected.

2. Make appointment to diagnose problem and determine time and materials likely to be needed.

3. Drive to their house.

4. Answer the phone call and make an appointment.

5. Look at the problem and decide what is wrong.

6. Go to supply house and get parts.

7. Write down a parts needed list.

8. Make sure all needed tools are at hand to perform job.

9. Make appointment to perform work.

10. Explain to client what your charges are and about what you expect the total job to cost.

11. Decide how long it will take to perform the repair.

12. If it is a leak from a water line, let client know how long the water will be off.

13. If it's a waste problem, let client know how long it is likely to be before they can use the sink or lavatory or toilet that you are going to work on.

14. Perform the job.

15. Arrange for any help you might need.

16. Make up bill.

17. Get paid. (IMPORTANT! Always ask for a referral!)

18. Deposit check in business account.

19. Make entries in ledger showing costs, vehicle time, rentals, pay for helper if used, total charged and deposited, net income to date.

From that initial list, a second list showing proper sequencing, can be created:

1. Answer the phone call and make an appointment.

2. Ask what the problem is that they need corrected.

3. Make appointment to diagnose problem and determine time and materials likely to be needed.

4. Drive to their location.

5. Look at the problem and decide what is wrong.

6. Write down a parts needed list.

7. Make sure all needed tools are at hand to perform job.

8. Decide how long it will take to perform the repair.

9. Explain to client what your charges are and about what you expect the total job to cost.

10. If it is a leak from a water line, let client know how long the water will be off.

11. If it's a waste problem, let client know how long it is likely to be before they can use the sink or lavatory or toilet that you are going to work on.

12. Make appointment to perform work.

13. Go to supply house and get parts.

14. Arrange for any help you might need.

15. Perform the job.

16. Make up bill.

17. Get paid. (IMPORTANT! Always ask for a referral!)

18. Deposit check in business account.

19. Make entries in ledger showing costs, vehicle time, rentals, pay for helper if used, total charged and deposited, net income to date.

This second list is an actual sequence of how you would service a client. This is how your steno notebook is to be set up for the initial pages. Do this for all three businesses, just from your thoughts. Later, you will perform some simple research to further refine your thoughts and make the final determination of which business you should be in and how you will operate it.

Now is the time to seek other people's thoughts. Don't ask them whether or not you should go into your own business. In fact, if they start asking you why you want to or what makes you think you can do it, get away from them and seek someone else. What you want is for other people, preferably three or four, to look at your list and offer their suggestions. Take their best ideas and add them into your second list in the appropriate order. -   Make a third list incorporating those additional tasks in the proper sequence.

  For example, someone might suggest that before you quote a price in number nine of your second list, you should call the supply house and get your costs. Then you can do your mark-up, add your anticipated labor, and give the client your best estimate. To add this into your list, you start the list a second time, but when you get to number nine, you insert the phrase "call supply house for price quote." Then you move the rest of your list one number higher. What was number nine becomes number ten; what was ten becomes eleven and so forth. Again, have at least three people, preferably four, look at your list and offer suggestions for additions.

Section 4:

Tools

Next you have to consider needed tools. Each step in each notebook has a number. Go down the list for each one and use the following pages to note whatever tool may be needed for a particular step. For instance, item four on our example list is "drive to their location." To drive to the client, you will need a vehicle. On the list corresponding to that notebook number and item number, write "Vehicle." Just write it down; don't try to give a value or cost to the item. That will come later.

If you need more lines, use a sheet of standard notebook paper. Be sure to keep it in order with the correct steno notebook.

Notebook 1

1. _____
2. _____
3. _____
4. _____
5. _____
6. _____
7. _____
8. _____
9. _____
10. _____
11. _____
12. _____
13. _____
14. _____
15. _____
16. _____
17. _____
18. _____
19. _____
20. _____

Notebook 2

1. _____
2. _____
3. _____
4. _____
5. _____
6. _____
7. _____
8. _____
9. _____
10. _____
11. _____
12. _____
13. _____
14. _____
15. _____
16. _____
17. _____
18. _____
19. _____
20. _____

Notebook 3

1. _____
2. _____
3. _____
4. _____
5. _____
6. _____
7. _____
8. _____
9. _____
10. _____
11. _____
12. _____
13. _____
14. _____
15. _____
16. _____
17. _____
18. _____
19. _____
20. _____

When all three notebooks are as detailed as you can get them, it is time for your final decision. Take your time and carefully consider each one, imagining yourself performing the sequential tasks shown. One of the three will stand out in your mind as the best choice; it may not be your original idea.

At this point, honestly consider whether you have all the knowledge you need to start the business. If you don't really know enough about how to do the job, strongly consider working, even part-time, for someone in the business. Avoid any firm that wants you to sign a "No-Compete" clause in the hiring contract. The "No-Compete" agreement is a legal clause saying that you will not work in the given profession for a particular period of time after leaving their employment.

The key, before you actually begin your business, is to have evaluated your abilities and what you know of the local market and come to the conclusion as to which business is right for you. Remember: what is right for you is uniquely the product of your skills and abilities, coupled with your own willingness to do whatever it takes to run a business. This will probably mean working a lot of hours. If you need to keep your current job estimate how much time you will have available to devote to starting and growing your new business.

NOTE: If you're moonlighting, for Heaven's sake, don't compete with your boss! That's dishonest and you will quickly get a bad reputation. Clients will also expect you to charge less!

Step 4:

Scheduling

While you are planning your schedule, keep in mind that families need attention, as well. If you have a family, include time which is set aside just for them. Make sure they understand and agree with your anticipated working hours. It's better to compromise now than to meet stiff resistance later!

Your schedule should include at least one hour per working day for office work Monday through Thursday and two hours on Friday. If you neglect this, you are setting yourself up to fail even as the clientele and income grows. Of course, you may be working a completely different schedule than the standard work week and, if so, just remember to set aside one hour for each day you work and an extra hour one day per week.

The schedule should only show a seven-day week, because it is the basic plan that you consistently follow and it should be set up similar to the following:

Key to Abbreviations:

Job = salaried primary job

Rec = recreation

Fam = family

Rcds = office/bookkeeping/planning

Bus = your new business

Relax = personal time

Sun	Mon	Tues	Wed	Thurs	Fri	Sat
Off	7am Arise	7am Arise	7am Arise	7am Arise	7am Arise	7am Arise
	8am Job	8am Job	8am Job	8am Job	8am Job	8am Bus.
	5pm Rcds	5pm Rcds	5pm Rcds	5pm Rcds	5pm Rcds	All Day Bus
	6pm Bus.	6pm Bus	6pm Bus	6pm Bus	6pm Bus	7pm Off
	8pm Fam.	8pm Fam.	8pm Fam.	8pm Fam.	8pm Fam.	8pm Fam.
	9pm	9pm	9pm	9pm	9pm	9pm

	Rec.	Rec.	Rec.	Rec.	Rec.	Rec
	10pm Relax	10pm Relax	10pm Relax	10pm Relax	10pm Relax	10pm Relax
	11pm Bed	11pm Bed	11pm Bed	11pm Bed	11pm Bed	11pm Bed

The above table is an example only. You will have to decide what your schedule will be based on your unique situation. If you don't have a family, you must still set aside time to enjoy friends or just to go out and eat or take in a movie. The 9pm Rec. entry indicates recreation. You must always remember the adage "All work and no play makes Jack a dull boy." It will also make a budding business person too weary to be effective. When you actually perform the tasks of your new business, you want to be wide awake, cheerful and fully focused in order to maximize your effort and results.

   Based on the schedule above, the individual would have two hours per day during the week and eleven hours on Saturday to start and grow the business. This brings up exactly why it is so important in the beginning that you make out a schedule: it's too easy to just assume you're going to have lots of available time to devote to your venture. Unless you're being supported by someone else who can comfortably pay all the bills, this just isn't so. You will have to use time taken from some other part of your life to create your business. Time, like financial debt, can become an unmanageable overhead expense. Spend what you need to and not a moment more. If things work out, there will come a point in the future when you'll have all the time you need.

Step 5:

Overhead

Now you need to determine what overhead you are going to have to meet. Regardless how frugal you are, certain things are required for even the smallest venture. In the steno notebook for the business you've chosen, turn to the next clean page and set it next to you. What follows is a list of costs and requirements you must determine before deciding if you need to learn more before taking the big step. As you go through these, you will take notes for any special instructions and requests the client you speak with provides. Write the number of the item from the list that you are working on, and then write out the important details they provide.

These should be satisfied in order, and the answer to each one filled in before going to the next one. For each "Yes" answer, write the cost in the space provided next to that question and check the "notes" line if you have made notes in your steno notebook explaining any special details.

1. Occupational License:
    A. City
    (check one)   Yes__ No__
    Cost_____ Notes__
    B. County
    (check one)   Yes__ No__
    Cost_____ Notes__
    C. State
    (check one)   Yes__ No__
    Cost_____ Notes__

2. Specialty License:
    A. City
    (check one)   Yes__ No__
    Cost_____ Notes__
    B. County
    (check one)   Yes__ No__
    Cost_____ Notes__
    C. State
    (check one)   Yes__ No__
    Cost_____ Notes__

Frequently, there are requirements for licensing that include passing examinations, such as air conditioning or plumbing. These normally require licensing by the city, county and state, plus an occupational license to do business.

3. Business Name
   A. Doing Business As (DBA)
   (Check one) Yes__ No__
   Cost_____ Notes__

4. Special Regulations:
   A. Vehicle signs
   (check one) Yes__ No__
   Cost_____ Notes__
   B. Business zoning
   (check one) Yes__ No__
   Cost_____ Notes__
   C. Sales tax
   (check one) Yes__ No__
   Cost_____ Notes__
   D. Permits
   (check one) Yes__ No__
   Cost_____ Notes__
   E. Other
   (check one) Yes__ No__
   Cost_____ Notes__

5. Insurance:
   A. Business
   (check one) Yes__ No__
   Cost_____ Notes__

    B. Vehicle
        (check one)   Yes__ No__
        Cost_____ Notes__
    C. Worker's Comp
        (check one)   Yes__ No__
        Cost_____ Notes__

6. Federal Employer's Identification Number
    A. Required
        (check one)   Yes__ No__
        Notes__

    B. Use Social Security Number
        (Check one)   Yes__ No__
        Notes__

    This is added to help you understand that many sole operator type businesses can use the business person's social security number when performing work for or selling a product to another business. They have to be able to report to the IRS or other taxing agencies who they paid and how much. Our suggestion is that you obtain a Federal Employer's Identification Number, since every business will readily accept that in order to pay you. Your bank may also require you have one. It doesn't cost anything and is easy to obtain. Simply call the IRS and they will help you. You can also obtain this on line at:

www.irs.gov/businesses/small/article/0,,id=102766,00.html

You may feel incorporating is a way to protect yourself from financial responsibility if serious problems come up. Most sellers are going to require you to sign a personal responsibility note when buying on credit, so this is probably of no immediate value. Talk to an attorney to find out if you should be a corporation or a sole proprietorship.

7. Business Checking Account:
   a. Require proof of license in business name
      (check one) Yes___ No___
      Cost_____ Notes___
   B. Minimum deposit
      (check one) Yes___ No___
      Cost_____ Notes___
   C. Set up costs
      (check one) Yes___ No___
      Cost_____ Notes___

8. Vehicle:
    A. Personal
        (check one)   Yes__ No__
        Cost_____ Notes__
    B. Business
        (check one)   Yes__ No__
        Cost_____ Notes__

In this instance, using your personal vehicle for business is going to create a great deal of excess wear and tear on it. The IRS allows you to track the mileage used for business and charge it off at a specified rate when completing your tax return. This will quickly become tedious and you will find yourself trying to remember where you went on a given day to "catch up" your records. This leads to error and tax liabilities. If you have a vehicle you can designate as only for business, go to a car dealer and ask them to give you a written appraisal. You will want to show that to your tax accountant to determine depreciation.

A sign on the side of the vehicle will generally allow you to "write off" all the operating costs, including gas, for it. Again, talk to your accountant.

9. Bookkeeping Service:

   A. Needed
      (check one)   Yes__ No__
      Cost_____ Notes__

This is one that we highly recommend to you. They aren't expensive. Find one and discuss your business plans with them *before* you see your first client! Unless you are a competent accountant, this person will keep you out of a lot of trouble. You should purchase a ledger from your local office supply store (Office Max, for example) and read the instructions thoroughly. The financial part of the record keeping mentioned earlier in this manual can be readily accomplished in a Dome Weekly Bookkeeping Recorder book. Of course, there are computer software programs as well that are very user-friendly. You should make all the entries yourself and take a copy to your tax accountant once per month. Be certain all income and receipted payouts are in the book! In fact, there should not be any pay-outs without some type of receipt, even if it's just a hand written note with a signature and the seller's name printed on it legibly, along with the date and a brief description of the item or service paid for.

The reason it is so important for you to make the entries yourself is to thoroughly familiarize yourself with the process of record keeping, so that you are always fully aware of your financial condition. Doing this for yourself will also make it easier for you to instruct someone else how you want it done when you are able to hire office help.

10. Equipment and Tools:

    A. Power equipment
       (check one) Yes___ No___
       Cost_____ Notes___
    B. Hand tools
       (check one) Yes___ No___
       Cost_____ Notes___
    C. Office equipment
       (check one) Yes___ No___
       Cost_____ Notes___

This is an item you will have to research a bit. If you need more than one piece of equipment, check the "Notes" line and write in your notebook all the items you will need along with the cost of each. Do the same with hand tools, which includes any implement you will manually utilize in your business. For instance, a plumber will probably need wrenches, whereas a writer will need pencils. Add them up and place the total on the appropriate "Cost" line above. Be sure to include a computer under "Office equipment" in this section if you will need one. ***Keep your receipts for tax purposes!***

11. Business location:

    A. Home
       (check one) Yes__ No__
       Cost_____ Notes__

    B. Commercial
       (check one) Yes__ No__
       Cost_____ Notes__

If you plan to work from home, be certain you won't run afoul of local ordinances. Look back at item #4 concerning zoning. If you are required to use a designated commercial location, go ahead and check in the newspaper for rental locations that match your needs. Then write the monthly amount on the "Cost" line. Don't be concerned with the price; this is all preliminary and serves to create a plan to work from.

If you will work from home, you must select a space for your records to be maintained. Even if it is only a single shelf that you place your books on after writing in them on the kitchen table, it must be set aside solely for that purpose. ***Discuss this with your tax preparer or accountant, as there are requirements for space in your home which are utilized for business.***

Now for the next big step and further research: go back over the items you've indicated have a cost and look for ways to either get them for free or for a greatly reduced amount.

For the occupational license, it might be that another county has lower costs and less strict requirements. If so, find out if they will accept a PO Box as a business address. If they do, check your intended county location for your business to see if they permit reciprocity. This is a courtesy between counties that allows a person licensed in one county to work in another. If this is acceptable, it also eliminates the need for expensive commercial space. You may still need to arrange to park a vehicle somewhere other than your home, though, if you are in the type business that requires obvious work vehicles. In this case, look for a friend or relative who lives in an area that will permit parking such equipment. As a last resort, offer a legitimate business location owner a small fee to allow you to park on his property.

For the power equipment, look into renting or, if you aren't setting yourself up for a fast-paced completion on any particular job, hire temporary labor and use hand tools to begin. The temporary labor can be from a temporary labor provider, a relative, or just someone you can use on a job basis, without permanently hiring them. Most legitimate temporary labor agencies will include all the necessary taxes and other legal costs in the hourly rate they charge you. If you hire someone directly, you may have a certain amount they can be paid before you have legal liabilities; you may also "get around" any taxation, including workers' comp, by providing them with an IRS wages form 1099. This will usually require they have their own occupational license, insurance and workers' compensation insurance if your state requires it. There are also tax liabilities if you hire someone on a long-term basis, including income tax deductions and Social Security. This is once more a place where a good tax accountant will be invaluable. Ask them!

Go back to your notes on Worker's Compensation to be sure you keep this strictly legal. The fines can be devastating and they have people out every day looking for violators.

Step 6:

Set-Up Costs

After trimming all the costs as far as you can, it's time to total them up and see how much you need to go into business. Most likely, the costs are going to be minimal. A license, a location, insurance, transportation and a few tools will most likely be all you need to start. Whatever the total is, be sure you have it set aside to begin. As one successful entrepreneur pundit said to the author of this manual, "You can make a lot of money with junk." Whatever will get you started and last through a few jobs is probably going to be sufficient to begin serving clients and earning new money.

By going through all of the steps to this point, you have actually created a written list of what you will need to become a full-time operation and to grow into a successful venture with others working for you.

Write a dollar amount by each item based on the list you just completed and then total them.

1. _____
2. _____
3. _____
4. _____
5. _____
6. _____
7. _____
8. _____
9. _____
10._____
Total: _____

Step 7:

Setting Up

This is the final step before actually beginning to set up and operate your business. How much will you charge? The easy answer is that you will charge about what others in your area, in the same type business, are charging. Okay, but how did they arrive at their price?

Price is the total of all the costs, plus a reasonable profit. While this sounds simple, in reality it can become very complex when dealing with intangibles, depreciation, taxes and so forth. For the fledgling entrepreneur, there are a couple of short cuts. The first is, of course, as mentioned before, simply charge the same price as your competitors. The second is to ask questions. The most helpful place for getting straight answers is a supplier. Find a reasonably sized wholesaler or distributor and tell them you want to become a client of theirs, but you need some info to make sure you make a profit. Ask what the going rate is for whatever product or service you intend to offer.

Contact the local Chamber of Commerce and ask them for an approximate pricing structure for the business you've chosen. Often, they will not only provide you with a price range, they will happily share some strong demographics with you that will better identify your intended customer.

If all else fails at the start, use the following formula to decide what you should charge:

1. Materials + costs (tax, etc.) times 2.5.

    A. Example: you purchased a planter at wholesale and you are going to sell it to a customer. The planter costs you $10.00 and the sales tax rate is 6%.

    10.00 x .06 = .60, so the planter costs you $10.60.

$10.60 \times 2.5 = \$26.50$, so your selling price is $26.50.

2. For a service-only business (a consultant, for instance) the simplest way is to work out the hourly charge by adding all of your costs for a month, dividing by 220 and adding the amount you want to earn. For instance, your costs may be limited to a vehicle and gasoline, so you calculate you'll drive about 30 miles per day for 22 days a month (this is the figure to use to assume working 5 days a week and taking off on the weekends) and 10 hours each day. Let's say your car payment is $440 per month and you want to make $30 an hour. Dividing 440 by 22 equals $110 and dividing that by 10 hours per day is $11 per hour in costs. Add in the $30 an hour you want to earn and your hourly rate charged to clients would be $41.

Those figures are for example purposes only and don't take into account that most one-person start-up businesses will not work a 5-day week, but will use the hours they have available. That's okay- just use the same method to compute the cost per hour and add your desired hourly rate for income. Again, don't forget to arrange time for office work; that's important because getting behind on the details of accounting, bill paying, collections, government forms and so forth can quickly overwhelm you.

Now, don't forget that this is an example; you will have to use your local price and sales tax rate. The reason we suggest including the sales tax when you make the wholesale purchase is that it may keep you from having to collect sales tax from your customer. Check with your state department of revenue. If they say you can do it this way, believe me, it will save you many headaches at the start-up stage of business. If you do have to collect the tax, be sure to deposit it immediately in your account and keep a separate record showing the current total. ***DO NOT spend this money!*** Pay it the way you are instructed. Just like Worker's Compensation, the fines can easily destroy a fledgling business even as it is becoming successful.

Step 8:

Marketing

The next step is to create a business card. While it always seems the easy way is to simply go to an office supply store and order them, it is actually better to make your own.. Go to Avery.com on the internet and download the software for printing business cards (it's free). Then go to your local office supply store and buy a small pack of business card blanks. For about fifteen dollars, you can easily design and print out cards any way you desire. The advantage here is that you aren't locked in to a thousand cards you're not happy with. Experiment with the design. Search the internet for examples. It really isn't difficult and will let you create a unique identity.

The important items that must always be on a business card are who you are, what you business is, contact information, and some reason why a client should use you. In some ventures, just saying that you really show up or that you will be on time is almost enough by itself.

Once you have the initial design, make sure you print up at least twenty-five or so. Keep them on you at all times. You're going to give them out every chance you get. Later, as you become more experienced about what image best represents your company you can order professionally printed cards. For now, keep it simple, effective and cheap.

A little research now will go a long way toward keeping you on track, pursuing real opportunities instead of just spinning your wheels. Write down the names of several successful businesses that are selling the same product or service that you plan to sell. Now, start looking for their advertising and see who they are soliciting. Maybe that's the customer you want.

Say you plan to open a lawn care business and you aren't sure what you should go after, commercial or residential. Look in the local yellow pages and find out which one the soon-to-be competitors are emphasizing. Take the time to find out what they consider important to mention in their advertising, as well.

Dependent upon the business you are setting up, you may need to check newspapers, magazines, web pages, or any number of other media to find existing businesses like yours. Take the time to do it. There is no reason to re-invent the wheel; no matter how creative your idea is, you can bet it's already been done in some form.

ALWAYS REMEMBER: CUSTOMER REFERENCES ARE A POTENT MARKETING TOOL

- Never let a day pass without engaging in at least one marketing activity.
- Determine a percentage of gross income to spend annually on marketing.

A good rule of thumb here is to plan for a total of 10% of your gross business income to be spent on advertising. This will include business cards, vehicle signs, and any other advertising. Remember to keep it simple and cheap; you are a one-person business, not a mega corporation.

- Set specific marketing goals every year; review and adjust quarterly.
- Maintain a tickler file of ideas for later use.
- Carry business cards with you (all day, every day).
- Create a personal nametag or pin with your company name and logo on it and wear it at high visibility meetings.
- Join a local small business persons' club.
- Start every day with two cold calls.
- Read newspapers, business journals, and trade publications for new business openings, personnel appointments, and promotion announcements made by companies. Send your business literature to appropriate individuals and firms.
- Give your sales literature to your lawyer, accountant, printer, banker, temp agency, office supply salesperson, advertising agency, etc. (Expand your sales force for free!)
- Put your fax number on order forms for easy submission.
- Set up a fax-on-demand or e-mail system to easily distribute responses to company or product inquiries.

- Follow up on your direct mailings, email messages, and broadcast faxes with a friendly telephone call.
- Try using the broadcast fax or email delivery methods instead of direct mail. (Broadcast fax and email allows you to send the same message to many locations at once.)
- Use broadcast faxes or email messages to notify your customers of product service updates.
- Extend your hours of operation.
- Reduce response/turnaround time. Make reordering easy - use reminders. Provide preaddressed envelopes.
- Display product and service samples at your office.
- Remind clients of the products and services you provide that they aren't currently buying.
- Call and/or send mail to former clients to try and reactivate them.
- Take sales orders over the Internet.

Section 9:

At Last

Are your ready? Okay, let's set you up. One step at a time, using all the information you've gathered, Follow the steps below and check them off. If a step is one you don't have to do, check the line marked "Not needed."

1. Office

    Yes____ Not needed_____

2. Ledger

    Yes____ Not needed_____

3. Telephone

    Yes____ Not needed_____

4. Pens/pencils

   Yes____ Not needed_____

5. Business cards

   Yes____ Not needed_____

6. Vehicle

   Yes____ Not needed_____

7. License

   Yes____ Not needed_____

8. Bank account

Yes____ Not needed_____

9. Supplier

   Yes____ Not needed_____

10. Pricing

    Yes____ Not needed_____

11. Tools

    Yes____ Not needed_____

It's finally time to actually start your business. Each step below is important and should be performed in the order it is stated.

1. Call on at least 2 potential clients.
2. Make appointment
3. Keep appointment
4. Determine client's need (make notes).
5. Contact supplier for your cost
6. Project the number of hours you will require to perform work/provide item
7. Multiply hours times your hourly rate (You must have a minimum; typically, one hour is a standard)
8. Add selling price of material/item
9. Quote price
10. Get agreement
11. Explain cash or check upon completion/delivery
12. Perform job/deliver item
13. Accept payment
14. Ask for referral
15. Make deposit
16. Make entries in ledger.

Repeat these steps every day. Once every two weeks for the first year, go over this manual from beginning to end. That will keep you focused on the realities of your business, not wishful thinking. Stay with it, apply yourself just like you laid out in these pages and you can anticipate a comfortable life for yourself and your loved ones, regardless of what the future may hold.

www.ingramcontent.com/pod-product-compliance
Lightning Source LLC
Chambersburg PA
CBHW071820170526
45167CB00003B/1388